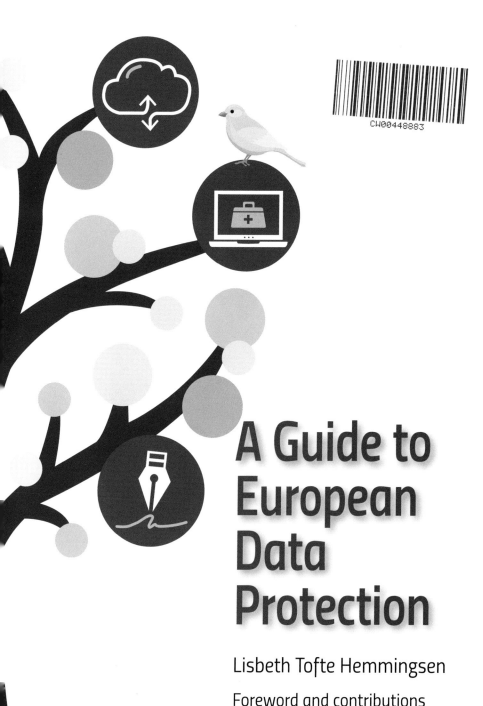

A Guide to European Data Protection

Lisbeth Tofte Hemmingsen

Foreword and contributions
by Professor David Hutchinson

Contents

Foreword

A new framework for data protection in Europe was adopted in April 2016, after a long and challenging development process. The new rules are implemented by the General Data Protection Regulation (No. 679/2016, the 'GDP Regulation'), which will replace the old data protection Directive 95/46/EC that was implemented into the laws of the EU Member States.

The GDP Regulation, which is effective from 25 May 2018, applies immediately to all European Economic Area countries, ie. to all EU Member States plus Norway, Lichtenstein and Iceland. The penalties for non-compliance are potentially very high – as much as 4% of a company's global turnover! It is therefore important that organizations have a good understanding of the requirements of the Regulation prior to its implementation, to ensure that they do not encounter any compliance issues.

This guide has been written by Lisbeth Tofte Hemmingsen, of Drug Safety Consult in Copenhagen, Denmark. She is an experienced quality assurance professional with many years' experience in the pharmaceutical and healthcare industries. She has broken down the Regulation into bite-sized chunks to make this difficult topic easy to understand. That in itself is a challenging task, but as you read this book I am sure you will appreciate the simplification.

Of course, there is no substitute for reading and absorbing the requirements of the Regulation itself. If you are a decision-maker, do make sure that you check any processes and procedures against the actual Regulation, and seek appropriate legal advice, prior to making organizational policies.

I hope that you enjoy reading this book and find it useful. Lisbeth, in conjunction with myself and Brookwood, has developed an online data protection training course that you may find interesting and informative. You can scan the QR code below to find out more about this.

Professor David Hutchinson

CHAPTER 1

Introduction

This guide to data protection covers the main elements of data privacy and the key obligations involved. It also describes the principles of the EU General Data Protection (GDP) Regulation that apply to all EU Member States. (A discussion of the detailed legal aspects of data protection is beyond the scope of this book.)

What is data protection?

Data protection (DP) is the safeguarding of personal data as required by law. It applies to all parties holding or accessing personal data.

What governs data protection?

Article 12 of the United Nations' Universal Declaration of Human Rights, issued in 1948, defines the right of individuals to the protection of their privacy by law. Today, the DP principles are laid down by the Organization for Economic Co-operation and Development and are further controlled by the national competent authorities through national legislation. In particular

- in the USA a sectoral approach is applied, combining legislation, regulation and self-regulation

- in the European Economic Area (EEA) the GDP Regulation (No. 679/2016) applies to all Member States.

It is important to be familiar with the general principles of DP and to be aware of the additional legal requirements that may apply in a specific country or region.

In this guide we will focus on the DP expectations laid down in the EU GDP Regulation. The Regulation has wide applicability and is not specific to the pharmaceutical sector. However, those aspects of DP relevant to pharmacovigilance and clinical trials are covered within this book.

Why is data protection important?

The privacy of our personal data is fundamentally important. Nevertheless, in our data-driven world there are numerous initiatives that require access to personal information in order to bring benefits to both individuals and society. A risk-based and balanced approach is therefore needed between the requirement for national (and cross-border) data flows and respect for personal privacy. The GDP Regulation has been designed to address both aspects.

NOTE:

Information on the DP rules in specific countries can be found in the annual worldwide data privacy overview compiled by the US Department of Health and Human Services' Office for Human Research Protections.

When thinking about DP in today's digital world, we need to consider

- the sheer volume of personal data being collected, used and stored

- the many analytics that use personal data to provide insights into trends, movement, interests and activities

- the benefits to society of the responsible use of personal data

- the extent of threats to privacy

- the large number of players involved

- the complexity of the interactions involving personal data that affect individuals

  - the global availability of personal data on multiple communication platforms.

The processing of personal data can bring benefits to humanity. An individual's control of their own personal data is therefore not an absolute right, but must be seen in the context of the data's function in wider society. DP has general applicability and is not specific to any sector. Its requirements must be balanced against the legislation that applies within a specific area. In this guide we will look at two examples that apply to the pharmaceutical industry:

- the need to balance data privacy rights against the obligation to oversee the safety of marketed products, as enforced by the EU Pharmacovigilance Regulation (No. 1235/2010)

- the need to collect health data in clinical trials during the development of medicines, as defined in the EU Clinical Trials Regulation (No. 536/2014).

CHAPTER 2

The EU GDP Regulation

The GDP Regulation has been introduced in the EU to ensure that personal data are protected. It is designed to provide a high level of protection, guaranteed by EU law, for natural persons (ie. the subjects to whom the personal data refer), economic operators and public authorities.

The Regulation allows for a consistent approach across all Member States, and removes obstacles to the flow of personal data between Member States within the EEA.

The Regulation states that personal data can be gathered legally only under strict conditions and for a legitimate purpose. Individuals or organizations collecting and managing personal data are required to protect the information from misuse and must respect the rights of the data owners.

The EU approach is considered to be a gold standard and to be the most comprehensive and progressive piece of DP legislation in the world. The GDP Regulation also applies to non-EU organizations and companies that offer goods and services to individuals in the EU or monitor their behaviour.

There are specific rules for the transfer of data to countries outside the EU, to ensure the protection of personal data when exported abroad. These are reflected in, for example, the EU–US Privacy Shield.

Businesses operating in the EU must observe the DP requirements. The huge fines for violating the DP rules are on a similar scale to those for anti-trust violations.

Two other pieces of legislation complement the GDP Regulation:

- Directive 2016/680, which governs the use of EU citizens' data by law enforcement agencies (eg. in preventing terrorism)

- the E-Privacy Regulation (replacing Directive 2009/136), also known as the 'cookie law', which supports a common digital market and regulates the use of apps and metadata to track consumer patterns.

Key roles

The key roles involved in DP are as follows:

- **Data Subject** – this is the person to whom the data refers. When this person is a natural person, DP legislation protects his/her rights. This should be seen in contrast to a *legal person* (eg. a person accused of a criminal offence), where the DP legislation does not apply to the same extent and public interests often prevail.

- **Data Controller** – this is the person/ institution/company who holds the data and is responsible for its protection.

- **Data Processor** – this is the person/ institution/company who processes the data on behalf of the Data Controller and is responsible for its correct and secure handling.

- **Data Protection Officer** – this is the person appointed by the Data Controller/Data Processor with the legal responsibility to oversee compliance with the requirements of the GDP Regulation and to act as a facilitator for the Data Subject's rights.

What are personal data?

Personal data are information concerning an identified or identifiable natural person, ie. someone who can be identified (directly or indirectly) by reference to an identifier.

An identifier can be a name, an identification number, location data or an online identifier. Identifiers can also be factors that are specific to the physical, physiological, genetic, mental, economic, cultural or social identity of the individual.

Certain types of data rate as sensitive personal data, and their processing is prohibited unless an exemption (derogation) applies. This includes personal data that reveal race or ethnic origin, political opinions, religion or beliefs, or trade union membership; and the processing of genetic data or data relating to health, sex life, criminal convictions or security measures.

Examples of sensitive personal data include

- genetic data relating to the inherited or acquired genetic characteristics of a natural person

- health data (ie. all data pertaining to the past, current or future physical or mental health status of the Data Subject).

The derogation can allow the processing of special categories of sensitive personal data where it is in the public interest to do so, and processing is subject to suitable safeguards. This can be for health security; for monitoring and alert purposes; for the prevention or control of diseases and other serious threats to health; or where it is necessary to exercise or defend legal claims.

NOTE:

Businesses that keep customer databases, lists of client e-mail addresses and similar personal data need to obtain permission from the Data Subjects, and should comply with the DP requirements in their handling of the data.

Where does it apply?

The GDP Regulation protects EU Data Subjects, and covers the processing of the personal data of EU Data Subjects by a Data Controller or Processor. It applies to Data Controllers and Processors whether or not they are located within the EU.

Where activities are outsourced to a third party, the overall responsibility for oversight and compliance remains with the original Data Controller or Processor.

Although personal data can be circulated without restrictions between Member States, any transfer to third-party countries is heavily regulated.

What is exempt?

The principles of DP do not apply to anonymous information. Anonymous information is information that does not relate to an identified or identifiable natural person, or information that is rendered anonymous in such a manner that the Data Subject is not or no longer identifiable.

Pseudonymized personal data, however, are not exempt (eg. encrypted data where the process can be reversed via an encryption key).

DP does not apply to personal data placed voluntarily on social media by the Data Subject. However, those providing the social media platform (eg. Facebook) are still obliged to follow the applicable DP legislation.

DP does not generally apply to the personal data of deceased persons. However, individual countries may have their own rules on this, so national law should be consulted.

Compliance

The European Data Protection Board (EDPB) oversees and monitors compliance with the DP requirements. The EDPB includes representatives from the Supervisory Authority (SA) that must be established in each Member State. The EDPB has its own powers and does not take instructions from any other entity.

A Member State SA is by law required to be independent. SAs are responsible for raising awareness about DP obligations and are authorized to investigate, detect and punish violations. Both Data Controllers and Processors must comply with the GDP Regulation and will be held accountable by the SA in case of infringement.

A 'one-stop-shop' principle requires a company to deal with the SA in one Member State only. The choice is based on the location of the company's main office. This single SA becomes the 'lead authority'. Where a processing activity affects Data Subjects in more than one Member State, the lead SA co-ordinates with all other affected SAs and the EDPB, to ensure that any enforcement action is consistent across the EU.

CHAPTER 3

Obtaining Personal Data

Any personal data that are collected should be adequate, relevant and limited to what is necessary for the purposes of processing ('data minimization').

For personal data to be processed, at least one of the following must apply as the legal basis:

- the Data Subject has given consent to the processing of his or her personal data for one or more specific purposes

- processing is necessary to execute a contract to which the Data Subject is party or where the Data Subject requests steps to be taken prior to entering into a contract

- processing is necessary for the Data Controller to comply with a legal obligation

- processing is necessary to protect the interests of the Data Subject or another natural person

- processing is necessary to perform a task carried out in the public interest (or is an official obligation of the Data Controller)

- processing is necessary for legitimate interests pursued by the Data Controller or by a third party, except where the interests or fundamental rights and freedoms of the Data Subject override such interests.

Consent

Explicit consent must be given by the Data Subject for the collection and processing of personal data. The giving of consent should be a clear affirmative act, and the consent must be freely given, specific and informed.

The Data Subject's consent must unambiguously indicate their agreement to the processing of personal data relating to him or her, such as in a written statement (including by electronic means) or oral statement.

The principle of transparency requires that any information addressed to the Data Subject is concise, easily accessible, easy to understand, and in clear and plain language.

Children merit specific protection. Where a data processing request is addressed to a child, the information should be in language that the child can easily understand. Parental consent is advised for children below 16 years of age and must be obtained for those under 13 years of age (for 16–13 year-olds the local legislation should be consulted).

In addition:

- if consent is requested electronically, the request must be clear, concise and not unnecessarily disruptive

- the specific purposes for which the personal data will be processed should be explicit, legitimate and determined at the time of collection

  - when the processing has multiple purposes, consent should be given for all of these

- the consent should cover all processing activities carried out for the same purpose(s)

- processing for new purposes is allowed only where it is compatible with the initial purposes; if it is not, new consent will be required.

When personal data are collected for scientific research, the purpose of data processing cannot always be identified at the time of data collection. Therefore, Data Subjects should be allowed to consent to certain areas of scientific research or to parts of research projects.

Rights of Data Subjects

Natural persons should have control of their own personal data and the protection of the Data Subject is considered to be a basic right. However, it is not an absolute right and must be seen in relation to the use of personal data to protect public interests.

Data Subjects have the right

- to be informed
- to access their data
- to have their data rectified or blocked
- to have their data erased (be forgotten)
- to move their data (portability).

Natural persons should be made aware of the risks, rules, safeguards and rights that relate to the processing of their personal data. They should be informed about how to exercise their rights and how to make a complaint to the SA.

Data Subjects have the right to withdraw their consent at any time without giving a reason, and without adverse consequences.

Obligations towards Data Subjects

Before any personal data are collected, the Data Controller should provide the Data Subject with information that includes the following:

- the identity and the contact details of the Data Controller and Data Protection Officer

- the purpose(s) of the processing

- the legal basis for the processing

- the recipient or categories of recipients of the personal data

- the length of time that the personal data will be stored

- the right to request from the Data Controller access to and rectification or erasure of the personal data

- the right to withdraw their consent at any time

- the right to make a complaint to the SA.

The Data Controller must be able to prove that consent has been obtained, and specifically that Data Subjects have consented to the various parts of data collection and processing. Records should document the consent process, showing how, why and for what consent was given.

Rights to the erasure of personal data mean that the Data Controller can be required to delete a Data Subject's personal data, and to take all reasonable steps to tell third parties to do the same. There are exceptions to this, such as where processing is necessary for reasons of public interest (eg. for public health, or for scientific or historical research purposes).

Data portability gives Data Subjects the right to receive their personal data in a commonly used and machine-readable format, and to transmit these data to another organization. This is not an unrestricted right: data portability should not adversely affect the rights and freedoms of others.

The Data Controller should establish processes that allow Data Subjects to exercise their rights. This includes mechanisms for Data Subjects to request – and, if applicable, to obtain free of charge – access to and the rectification or erasure of personal data, and to object to their data being held.

The Data Controller should enable Data Subjects' requests to be made electronically, especially where personal data are processed electronically. The Data Controller must respond to these requests without undue delay (within 1 month) and must give reasons if they do not intend to comply with the requests.

NOTE:

Where processing is based on the Data Subject's consent, the Data Controller should be able to demonstrate that the Data Subject has given consent to the processing operation and has been informed about personal data retention times and the contact details of the Data Controller and Data Protection Officer.

Risk assessment

The Data Controller must assess the impact of the proposed data processing. This involves considering the risks to the personal data and how these will be mitigated. Where new technologies will involve a high risk, the impact assessment must consider the nature, scope, context and purposes of the processing.

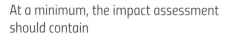

At a minimum, the impact assessment should contain

- a description of the processing operations and purpose

- an assessment of the necessity and proportionality of the processing

- an assessment of the risks to Data Subjects

- details of the measures that will be taken to address the risks (including safeguards, security measures and mechanisms to ensure the protection of personal data) and to demonstrate compliance.

The prior approval of the DP authorities is required where there are specific risks to the rights and freedoms of Data Subjects.

NOTE:

To comply with the GDP Regulation, Data Controllers and Processors may need to enter into new agreements with their service providers or to find new system solutions. An up-to-date and precise inventory of the personal data that are controlled/processed may be useful.

Transfer outside EEA

Companies are prohibited from transferring personal data out of the EEA, unless

- the transfer is to an adequate jurisdiction (ie. one declared by the EU Commission to adequately protect personal data)

- the transfer is ensured by an adequate level of protection using standard contractual (model) clauses adopted by the EU Commission or an approved DP agency, or

- a derogation applies.

A derogation allows the transfer of personal data to a third country or an international organization if

- it is not on a large scale or frequent

  - it is necessary for the purposes of the Data Controller's legitimate interests, which are not overridden by the interests (or rights and freedoms) of Data Subjects

- the Data Controller has assessed the circumstances surrounding the data transfer operations and confirmed that there are suitable safeguards for the protection of personal data.

NOTE:

Companies must consider DP when implementing new technology or deciding on the location of cloud computing solutions. For EU personal data the preference is for cloud solutions located within the EU; this is best addressed in the contract with providers.

CHAPTER 4

Controlling and Processing Personal Data

Record keeping

Companies need to use self-verification tools and must maintain records to ensure that their existing compliance programmes follow the requirements of the GDP Regulation.

Data Controllers must demonstrate that personal data processing is performed in compliance with the Regulation. Mechanisms must be implemented to ensure that personal data are only processed when necessary for each specific purpose.

Data Controllers should keep clear records of all personal data processing activities. The records must also document compliance with requests for the removal and destruction of, and access to, data. Data Processors are also legally obliged to maintain records of personal data processing activities and must implement appropriate information security measures.

Any restrictions relating to cross-border data transfers must be complied with.

The written approval of the Data Controller is required for subcontracting processing activities or enlisting other Data Processors. The Data Processor must inform the Data Controller immediately if a breach of personal data is discovered.

The Data Protection Officer

Companies will need to appoint a Data Protection Officer if the number of employees exceeds 250, if the core activities of the Data Controller or Processor require the regular and systematic monitoring of Data Subjects on a large scale, or if there is processing of sensitive personal data on a large scale.

There may be additional local reasons for the appointment of a Data Protection Officer – national law should be consulted.

The company must provide sufficient resources for the Data Protection Officer, who will

- be responsible for overseeing DP

- maintain detailed knowledge of DP law and practices

- keep company management informed about their obligations

- be the primary contact point for SAs

- be involved in all areas of DP within the organization

  - be notified of all data processing and protection issues or concerns in a timely manner

  - ensure that DP policies and procedures are updated

- ensure that staff are appropriately trained and responsibilities are assigned

- act as the advocate for Data Subjects asserting their right to control the data that describes them.

NOTE:

In practice, every company would benefit from having an individual or a governance group to oversee compliance with the GDP Regulation.

Data protection 'by design and default'

The phrase 'by design and by default' in the GDP Regulation means that DP should be designed into the development of business processes. The protection of personal data 'by default' means that the strictest privacy settings automatically apply for any new products or services.

For each new service or business process that makes use of personal data, companies need to show that

- adequate security is in place
- compliance is monitored
- means to verify the integrity of personal data have been implemented.

Personal data must be protected from destruction, loss and alteration, and from unauthorized disclosure, dissemination or access. Privacy settings must be set at a high level by default, and technical and procedural measures and organizational processes must be implemented to ensure compliance throughout the whole processing lifecycle.

All procedures for handling personal data must be documented.

Encryption and decryption operations are best carried out locally, not by remote services, as both the decryption key and the data must remain under the control of the Data Controller. Data storage on remote clouds is safer if the cloud service does not hold the decryption key.

NOTE:

Systems must be set up to ensure the protection of personal data, and IT infrastructure must be designed with the legislation in mind. In practice this implies that an IT department must take DP into account during the whole lifecycle of system or process development.

Data storage

The storage period for personal data is limited to a strict minimum. To ensure that personal data are not kept for longer than necessary, the Data Controller should establish time limits for erasure or for periodic review.

Processing should be in a manner that ensures appropriate security and confidentiality. Unauthorized access to or use of personal data, or to the equipment used for its processing, must be prevented. Any requests for access to, or for the removal and destruction of, data should be documented.

Every reasonable step should be taken to ensure that inaccurate personal data are rectified or deleted.

Records of processing activities must be maintained and must include the purposes of the processing, the categories involved and the envisaged time limits. These records must be made available to SAs on request.

Data audits

Data audits will be carried out on behalf of SAs by accredited certified bodies. Documentation on processing activities, and on the consent process and the provision of full information to Data Subjects, will need to be readily available.

To ensure that they are prepared for an audit, Data Controllers and Processors should

- consider DP in all technology, products or services that involve the processing of personal data

- review existing compliance programmes to ensure compliance

- ensure that full documentation of Data Subjects' consent is available

- ensure that there are clear records of all data processing activities

- establish a plan for addressing any gaps

- allocate clear responsibilities for each step

- train personnel on the requirements of the GDP Regulation and maintain training records.

Data breaches, compensation and penalties

Where the GDP Regulation has not been complied with, Data Subjects who have suffered damage caused by the processing of their personal data are entitled to compensation from the Data Controller or Processor.

Data Controllers and Processors must ensure that the appropriate measures are in place to establish immediately whether a personal data breach has taken place, and to promptly inform the SA and Data Subject. The Data Controller must inform the SA without delay and within 72 hours if a breach of personal data

NOTE:

Data Controllers must have monitoring and reporting systems in place to ensure that breaches are identified as soon as possible, and to help protect the integrity of data. Data Controllers and Processors will need to establish procedures to enable a prompt response in the event of a breach of personal data.

involves a risk to individuals' rights and freedoms. The Data Subject must also be informed without delay.

If a DP Officer has been appointed, s/he is responsible for monitoring, notifying and otherwise communicating information about personal data breaches.

According to the GDP Regulation, the following sanctions can be imposed by SAs:

- a written warning for first and non-intentional non-compliance

- regular periodic DP audits

- fines.

Fines take the form of a fixed sum or a percentage of the company's annual worldwide turnover for the preceding financial year, whichever is greater. A fine of up to €10 million or up to 2% of turnover will apply where Data Controllers and Processors

- do not maintain a record of data processing activities

- fail to provide certain information to Data Subjects

- do not report data breaches

- do not carry out data impact assessments.

A fine of up to €20 million or up to 4% of turnover will apply where Data Controllers and Processors

- perform data processing with no legal basis

- fail to inform Data Subjects, fail to provide access for Data Subjects or do not rectify data

- do not erase personal data

- carry out or instruct data transfers in violation of the GDP Regulation.

CHAPTER 5

Data Protection and Pharmacovigilance

The safeguarding of public health is in the public interest. The processing of personal data for pharmacovigilance purposes is therefore justified, as long as identifiable personal data are only processed where necessary. This needs to be assessed at every stage of the pharmacovigilance process.

Data relating to the health of a patient are generally considered to be sensitive personal data. When carrying out pharmacovigilance, marketing authorization holders routinely collect health-related information to ensure the safety of patients and to comply with their obligations to report suspected adverse reactions to the regulatory authorities.

Consent

Data Subjects' right to DP must be fully and effectively guaranteed in all pharmacovigilance activities.

Pharmacovigilance data may include personal data and sensitive personal data related to the patient, as well as personal data related to the reporter (who may be the patient's healthcare provider, family member or the patient themselves).

Whether the Data Subject is the patient who experienced an adverse reaction or the person reporting the case, it is *not necessary to obtain consent* for the reporting of pharmacovigilance data or for the processing of personal data. However, Data Subjects should be informed if their personal data are being collected, and by whom and for what purposes.

Data Subjects can object to their personal data being processed. However, to fulfil their pharmacovigilance obligations, marketing authorization holders are required by law to collect certain minimum information on individuals who experience an adverse reaction to a medicinal product. Marketing authorization holders are therefore not obliged to comply with Data Subjects' objections when processing personal data for pharmacovigilance. Nevertheless, they must comply with the GDP Regulation and put transparent and robust processes into place to ensure that personal data are protected and the rights of Data Subjects are supported.

Data security and storage

Specific measures should be taken at each stage in data processing and storage to ensure data security and confidentiality. Access to documents and databases should be strictly limited to authorized personnel.

The need for anonymization should be considered for data transfer solutions, and sensitive personal data should be encrypted to ensure the integrity of data transmissions.

Companies should be able to justify why they retain data for a specific period, eg. as required by the pharmacovigilance legislation.

Data minimization should be adopted to identify the minimum amount of personal data needed to properly fulfil the safety reporting obligations. A company should not de-identify or redact personal data if its pharmacovigilance obligations are compromised by doing so.

Appropriate structures and processes must ensure that pharmacovigilance data and records are protected from destruction during the applicable record retention period. Any database containing personal data should be fully validated or tested to ensure that changes to data can be identified (audit trail) and access is restricted to named individuals.

The location of DP compliance documentation should meet the requirements of both the DP Officer and the Pharmacovigilance Master File.

NOTE:

Documented training in DP requirements is recommended for all company staff involved in pharmacovigilance activities.

CHAPTER 6

Data Protection and Clinical Trials

The health data collected in clinical trials – including biometric and genetic data – are sensitive personal data and the requirements of the GDP Regulation will need to be considered for all planned or ongoing trials.

Pseudonymized data count as personal data; only anonymized data are excluded from the requirements of the GDP Regulation.

Consent

Explicit, unambiguous and freely given consent is required both by Good Clinical Practice (GCP) and the GDP Regulation.

Combining the information required by the GDP Regulation with the information required by GCP could result in very lengthy consent forms. Data Controllers (sponsors) should consider ways to balance the amount of information given with the patient's ability to understand it, seeking to simplify the message whilst ensuring compliance with both sets of requirements.

Where medical research projects rely on the integrity of the personal data that were originally collected and processed, these data will normally be exempt if a Data Subject withdraws their consent. The withdrawal will only apply to future data collection and processing. However, data may only be kept if there is a legal basis for doing so. Where there is no legal basis for justifying the further storage of such personal data after the withdrawal of consent, these data should be deleted wherever they are stored.

In Europe, the legal basis is laid down in the EU Clinical Trials Regulation (No. 536/2014). Article 58 requires the sponsor to archive the clinical trial documents and data for at least 25 years from the end of a trial. European Member States will specify how long institutions (ie. investigators) will have to keep their data and national rules should therefore be consulted.

All organizations involved in clinical trials should maintain documented evidence of any DP consents obtained and of the steps taken to comply with the GDP Regulation.

Obligations

The GDP Regulation allows for the appointment of joint Data Controllers (or co-sponsors, as allowed by the Clinical Trials Regulation) and also imposes obligations on Data Processors (ie. contract research organizations, investigators or statisticians). It must therefore be clear who is responsible for what and for how long.

As clinical trials involve the processing of sensitive personal data, a DP impact assessment will be needed for forthcoming trials, and for ongoing trials where no assessment has been performed. For activities completed prior to the enforcement of the GDP Regulation, the legislation should be consulted.

NOTE:

Documented evidence of DP consents will probably need to be kept in the Trial Master File, to demonstrate compliance with the applicable laws.

Care needs to be taken in the transfer of personal data from electronic media (eg. hospital electronic patient records). It can be challenging to document compliance with the GDP Regulation both for those data that are collected and those remaining behind.

The transfer of personal data from clinical trials to sponsors and other service providers (eg. contract research organizations) located outside the EEA is prohibited unless the conditions of the GDP Regulation are fulfilled.

NOTE:

Where identifiable data are not required they should be anonymized, eg. before they are accessed for secondary research or clinical audit purposes. When irrevocably anonymized, the data can no longer be linked to an individual and therefore no longer constitute personal data.

QUIZ

Test your knowledge

1. **In what circumstances does the EU General Data Protection (GDP) Regulation apply?**
   Choose 3 answers.

   A) Data protection is an absolute right

   B) Data protection is not an absolute right but must be seen in context with other rights

   C) The GDP Regulation is not linked to any specific business

   D) The GDP Regulation does not apply to the pharmaceutical industry

   E) The GDP Regulation does not cover data obtained before 2018

   F) The GDP Regulation applies to companies/businesses located outside the EU if they are dealing with EU data

2. **According to the GDP Regulation, which of the following statements are correct?** Choose 2 answers.

   A) A Data Subject is responsible for managing user accounts to personal PCs

   B) A Data Subject is subject to severe punishment if they leak their data

   C) A Data Subject is the person to whom the personal data refer

   D) A Data Subject is a living person

   E) A Data Subject is a registered taxpayer from a non-EU country

3. **True or false?**
   Personal data are information on an identified or identifiable person.

4. **True or false?**
   The GDP Regulation also applies to people after they have died.

Answers on page 33.

5. **Which statements about sensitive personal data are correct?**
Choose 2 answers.

A) They can be kept for an unlimited period of time

B) They can be collected freely if not exported outside the EU

C) They can only be collected under strict conditions and for legitimate purposes

D) They can be exported freely if encrypted

E) They can only be exported under strict conditions

6. **Where does the GDP Regulation apply?** Choose 3 answers.

A) To businesses operating in the EU

B) To businesses located abroad and importing EU products

C) To businesses exporting goods to the European Economic Area

D) To businesses processing or holding data on EU citizens

E) To businesses monitoring EU citizens' behaviour

7. **True or false?**
A company in India must comply with the GDP Regulation if processing EU personal data.

8. **What are sensitive personal data?**
Choose 2 answers.

A) Data on religion or political opinions

B) Data placed by the individual on social media

C) Statements made by politicians

D) Data on the health status of the individual

E) Telephone numbers

9. **Which statements about consent are correct?** Choose 2 answers.

A) It should be freely given

B) It can be obtained at any stage during data processing

C) It should be renewed on an annual basis

D) It can be obtained collectively to cover a group of people (eg. a family)

E) Parental consent must always be obtained for a child below 13 years of age

10. **Which statements about Data Subjects are correct?** Choose 3 answers.

    A) They have the right to access their data

    B) They should be informed about the legal basis for the processing of personal data

    C) They can require their data to be backed up on a separate server

    D) They can require their data to be stored forever

    E) They can withdraw their consent at any time

11. **Which statements about Data Controllers are correct?** Choose 2 answers.

    A) They oversee the allocation of user IDs to the network

    B) They must personally witness that consent is correctly obtained

    C) They are legally responsible for the correct handling of the personal data obtained

    D) They must establish a process that allows for Data Subjects to exercise their rights

    E) They can only hold personal data that do not affect the rights and freedoms of individuals

12. **Which statements about the privacy impact assessment are correct?** Choose 2 answers.

    A) It must consider how risks to Data Subjects can be addressed

    B) It is only needed for sensitive personal data

    C) It covers all the steps in the processing of data

    D) It is an internal document that never needs prior approval by the data protection authorities

    E) It must be signed off by all involved Data Processors

13. **Which statements about Data Protection Officers are correct?** Choose 3 answers.

    A) They monitor the behaviour of Data Subjects

    B) They have detailed knowledge of the data protection requirements

    C) The Data Protection Officer is the only person who can access personal data

    D) They ensure that staff are trained in data protection requirements

    E) The Data Protection Officer is the contact person for the Supervisory Authorities

31

Answers on page 33.

14. True or false?
Personal data can be circulated freely to third-party countries, if encrypted.

15. True or false?
Client e-mail lists are not protected data.

16. Which statements about non-compliance with the GDP Regulation are correct?
Choose 2 answers.

A) The health authorities will perform regular audits for compliance

B) A Data Protection Officer must oversee and communicate any personal data breaches

C) A personal data breach must be announced immediately via the press

D) Only companies earning more than €2 million will be subject to penalties

E) The Supervisory Authority can impose fines for non-compliance

17. True or false?
Personal data from clinical trials can be kept for an unlimited amount of time.

18. Which statements about data storage are correct?
Choose 3 answers.

A) Data Processors should keep a back-up copy of all personal data that are destroyed

B) Any processing must be carried out in a secure and confidential manner

C) There are no time limits on the storage of personal data

D) Records of processing activities must be maintained

E) Inaccurate personal data should be deleted

19. Which statements about records of data processing activities are correct? Choose 3 answers.

A) They must include the purpose of processing

B) They can be deleted once the processing has taken place

C) They should capture all access to the personal data

D) They are confidential and not available for audit

E) They cover all categories of personal data processed

20. True or false?
Consent from the Data Subject is required in all circumstances.

ANSWERS

Answers to quiz

1.	B, C, F	8.	A, D	15.	False
2.	C, D	9.	A, E	16.	B, E
3.	True	10.	A, B, E	17.	False
4.	False	11.	C, D	18.	B, D, E
5.	C, E	12.	A, C	19.	A, C, E
6.	A, D, E	13.	B, D, E	20.	False
7.	True	14.	False		

Data Protection Checklist

- ☐ Check which types of data you have.
- ☐ Are they protected data?
- ☐ Are they sensitive personal data?
- ☐ Which data do you need to keep? Don't keep more than necessary.
- ☐ For how long do you need to keep the data? Don't keep them for longer than needed or required.
- ☐ Where are the data? Is the documentation of this sufficient?
- ☐ Who can access the data? Limit access to a few named individuals.
- ☐ Is it a legal option to anonymize all or some of the data without obscuring their purpose?
- ☐ Are the data kept on secure media?
- ☐ Are the data backed up at a known location (eg. a storage cloud in the EU)?
- ☐ Have you obtained individuals' consent to their personal data being held, for the applicable length of time?
- ☐ Have national/non-EU requirements been considered?
- ☐ Are all steps documented?
- ☐ Is a response plan in place to enable a prompt response in the event of a data breach?